THE CASE OF THE
Hungry
Stranger

An I Can Read Book®

THE CASE OF THE
Hungry
Stranger

Story and pictures by Crosby Bonsall

HarperCollins*Publishers*

HarperCollins®, 🐾®, and 1 Can Read Book®
are trademarks of HarperCollins Publishers Inc.

THE CASE OF THE HUNGRY STRANGER
Copyright © 1963, 1992 by Crosby Bonsall
Manufactured in China. All rights reserved.
For information address HarperCollins Children's Books,
a division of HarperCollins Publishers, 10 East 53rd Street, New York, NY 10022
Newly Illustrated Edition

Library of Congress Cataloging-in-Publication Data
Bonsall, Crosby Newell, date
    The case of the hungry stranger / by Crosby Bonsall.
      p.   cm. — (An I can read book)
    Summary: Wizard and his friends are clueless when they are sent on
the trail of a blueberry pie thief, until Wizard hits on a plan that
is sure to nab the sweet-toothed pilferer.
    ISBN 0-06-020570-9. — ISBN 0-06-020571-7 (lib. bdg.)
    ISBN 0-06-444026-5 (pbk.)
    [1. Mystery and detective stories.] I. Title. II. Series.
PZ7.B64265Cas 1992   91-13345
[E]—dc20   CIP
                        11 12 13 SCP 30 29 28   AC

They all sat

in the clubhouse.

Wizard and Tubby,

Skinny and Snitch.

6

Wizard was the leader.

Tubby was his pal.

Skinny was his pal.

Snitch was his little brother.

Wizard knew a lot,

so he was called Wizard.

Tubby ate a lot,

so he was called Tubby.

Skinny did not eat a lot,

so he was called Skinny.

Snitch was called Snitch

because he told on his brother.

Sometimes.

9

The clubhouse was under a tree,

by a brook,

near a fence,

in Wizard's backyard.

There was an old sign on the door.

It said: NO GIRLS

There was a new sign on the door.

It said: THE WIZARD

PRIVATE EYE

"What is a private eye?"

asked Snitch.

"I am a private eye," said Wizard.

"I find things."

"I lost a penny once," said Snitch.

Wizard said, "I don't find lost things.

I find things that have been taken.

If someone took your penny,

I would find out who took it

and get it back for you."

"Free?" asked Snitch.

"For a nickel," said Wizard.

"Let it stay lost," said Snitch.

"You have to be sharp

to be a private eye," Wizard said.

"You have to keep your eyes open."

He looked at Snitch.

"You have to keep your mouth closed."

14

Mrs. Meech, the lady next door,

ran across the yard.

"Which one of you ate

my blueberry pie?" she asked.

They all looked at Tubby.

Mrs. Meech said,

"I baked two pies.

I put them out to cool.

And someone ate one.

All that is left is an empty pie plate."

"I didn't eat it," said Wizard.

"I didn't eat it," said Tubby.

"I didn't eat it," said Skinny.

"I didn't eat it," said Snitch.

"Cross my heart."

Mrs. Meech said,

"I need a private eye."

"You came to the right place,"

said Wizard.

"We'll find out

who ate the pie."

"I am sure you will," said Mrs. Meech.

Wizard looked at the boys.

"We will start right here," he said.

"Tubby, where were you

before you came here?"

19

"I went to the store

for a loaf of bread for Mom,"

Tubby said.

"I got some cookies for me, too."

"Where were you, Skinny?"

asked Wizard.

20

"I was watching my little sister

while my mother hung up the clothes,"

Skinny said.

"Where were you, Snitch?"

asked Wizard.

Snitch looked funny.

"I was with you," he said.

Now Wizard looked funny.

"Where were YOU, Wizard?"

asked Tubby and Skinny.

They climbed the fence.

They walked across the grass.

They stopped at Mrs. Meech's

back door.

The pie plate was on a bench.

It was empty, all right.

"I'll tell," said Snitch.

"It's funny.

Mom was trying on her new hat."

"That's not so funny,"

said Tubby and Skinny.

"She was trying it on Wizard,"

cried Snitch.

24

"THAT'S FUNNY!"

cried Tubby and Skinny

"Come on, men," Wiza

"We have to look

for fingerprints, and fo

and anything else that

25

"Here's a footprint," yelled Skinny.

"It looks new," Wizard said.

Then he looked at Skinny's feet.

"It's YOUR footprint," he yelled.

"You just made it!"

Tubby was looking at

the open cellar door.

"Maybe he went down here,"

he said.

"I'll go look."

The cellar was very dark.

It was damp and still.

Tubby fell over something.

It was soft. It moved.

It seemed to grab him.

"Help!" cried Tubby.

"I've got him!"

Mrs. Meech put on the light.

And there was Tubby

all tied up in the garden hose.

"You're a dope,"

said Wizard.

Outside, Wizard had a few things
to say to all of them.
"We are not getting very far
with this case," he said.
"Hey, here's a pie crumb," yelled Snitch.

31

"That means he went that way,"

cried Wizard.

"Let's go."

They followed the crumbs

across the grass,

up to the fence.

They saw the crumbs again

across the brook.

"Don't make a sound,"

said Wizard. "I think we've got him."

Tubby ate a cookie.

But he did not make a sound.

The trail led to the tree

and then to the door

of the clubhouse.

"S-sh," said Wizard,

"I'll open the door fast.

We'll catch him red-handed!"

There was no one there.

"Shucks, he got away,"

said Skinny.

"We almost had him," said Tubby.

He ate another cookie.

Some cookie crumbs fell

on the grass.

They all looked at the crumbs.

"Those were cookie crumbs

we followed," Wizard said.

"Tubby's old cookie crumbs,"

said Skinny.

"We must find out who did it,"
Wizard said.

"We can't be private eyes
if we don't find out
who ate the blueberry pie,"
said Skinny.

"Blueberry pie," said Wizard.

"Blueberry pie," said Wizard again.

"Hey, let me see your teeth."

"Why?" asked Tubby.

"Just let me see your teeth," said Wizard.

"And you can see mine."

39

"What do teeth

have to do with it?"

Skinny asked.

"I lost one," said Snitch.

"Does that count?"

"No," said Wizard.

"But if we had eaten

that blueberry pie,

our teeth would be blue!"

"And our teeth aren't blue,"

cried Tubby and Skinny.

"I think the one I lost was blue,"

said Snitch.

"Let's each go out alone,"
said Wizard, "and look for
someone with blue teeth."

42

They went up and down the block.

They went to each house.

They smiled and they smiled.

Snitch smiled at the mailman.

The mailman smiled back.

But his teeth were not blue.

Tubby smiled at

the ice-cream man.

The ice-cream man smiled back.

But his teeth were not blue.

And Tubby got an ice-cream cone.

Skinny smiled at

the paper boy.

The paper boy smiled back.

But his teeth were not blue.

45

Wizard smiled at

the policeman.

The policeman smiled back.

Of course his teeth were not blue!

Wizard and Tubby and Skinny

met back at the clubhouse.

"I didn't see one blue tooth,"

Skinny said.

"Where's Snitch?" asked Wizard.

No one knew.

"I told Mom I'd watch him,"

Wizard said.

"Let's go look for him."

But they didn't have to look.

48

Snitch came running

across the yard.

"Hurry," he said. "Hurry!

I have found the blue teeth!"

They all ran after Snitch.

They jumped across the brook.

They climbed the fence.

They ran across the grass.

Mrs. Meech was weeding.

She looked up and smiled.

Every one of her teeth was blue!

"Aw, Snitch," said Wizard.

"Her teeth are blue," said Snitch.

"They are indeed, Snitch,"

said Mrs. Meech.

"I had a dish of blueberries

for my lunch."

Back at the clubhouse

Wizard had a few things to say to Snitch.

"But you said to look for

blue teeth," Snitch said.

"Not Mrs. Meech's blue teeth,"

yelled Wizard.

Just then a dog ran

through a hole under the fence.

He jumped over the brook

and sat down beside them.

"Hey, he's been with us all day,"

Snitch said.

"He's a nice dog," said Skinny.

"Does he want a cookie?" asked Tubby.

54

The dog ran to Wizard.

He wagged his tail

and sat down.

Wizard smiled at the dog.

The dog smiled back at Wizard.

Then Wizard yelled.

Then they were all yelling.

The dog was barking.

He was jumping around.

And he was smiling.

The dog was smiling

a deep blue smile.

A blueberry pie smile.

"The case is closed," Wizard said.

"Here's our pie-eater.

Let's take him to Mrs. Meech."

The dog smiled his deep blue smile

at Mrs. Meech.

"You did a good job, boys,"

Mrs. Meech said.

"Now we're really private eyes,"

Wizard told her.

Someone cried, "Mop! Mop!"

A girl walked across the grass.

"There you are, Mop,"

she said to the dog.

"Where have you been all day?"

The dog just smiled.

But Wizard told her.

Tubby told her.

Skinny told her.

And Snitch told her.

He always told.

Mrs. Meech said,

"Would you like it? The blueberry pie

Mop didn't eat?"

Tubby was the first to say "Yes."

They took the pie

to the clubhouse.

Mop and the girl came, too.

The girl's name was Marigold.

She sat on the grass with them

and ate blueberry pie.

And they all smiled.

And each one of them smiled

a deep blue smile.